101 Awesome Bible Puzzles for Kids

Steve & Becky Miller

HARVEST HOUSE PUBLISHERS
EUGENE, OREGON

To you, the reader—
may you always find great joy
in exploring the Bible,
which is a lifelong adventure!

Acknowledgments

With appreciation to those at Harvest House Publishers who had a part in getting this book published and making it the best it can be, including Terry Glaspey, Betty Fletcher, Barb Gordon, Peggy Wright, Gary Lineburg, Chad Dougherty and Georgia Varozza.

Unless otherwise indicated, all Scripture quotations are from the Holy Bible, New International Version®, NIV®. Copyright © 1973, 1978, 1984 by Biblica, Inc.® Used by permission. All rights reserved worldwide.

Verses marked ICB are taken from the International Children's Bible®. Copyright © 1986, 1988, 1999 by Thomas Nelson, Inc. Used by permission. All rights reserved.

Verses marked NKJV are taken from the New King James Version®. Copyright © 1982 by Thomas Nelson, Inc. Used by permission. All rights reserved.

Cover by Koechel Peterson & Associates, Inc., Minneapolis, Minnesota

Cover illustration © totallyPic.com / Thinkstock

HARVEST KIDS is a registered trademark of The Hawkins Children's LLC. Harvest House Publishers, Inc., is the exclusive licensee of the federally registered trademark HARVEST KIDS.

The Old Testament

```
  J E R E M I A H M Y     L R O N U M B E R S
S O C M Z H P R O V E R B S U A F W A P X O L M
J B C D R O V K L Y U Z Q H T R P S L M J T E L
U A L Y A S R Q U A F P N E H E M I A H O L V S
D D E U T E R O N O M Y D S A R O G C X N S I G
G I S A I A H T M D Z E P H A N I A H P A I T N
E A I M B Q T Y N I E L N A T S M Z I O H C I L
S H A B A K K U K A C O M T E S T H E R D L C G
J O S H U A I D W T H A G G A I L S P U S W U E
K O T A L S N A R Q A U H D L T J T J S L I S N
G L E R M B G N E U R T M A L I I G H R A P A E
I P S L J U S I K M I F E R C H R O N I C L E S
E X O D U S E E T L A N X A L V S E N R K W M I
D E Z E K I E L G R H R J S O N G O F S O N G S
```

GENESIS	NEHEMIAH	HOSEA
EXODUS	ESTHER	JOEL
LEVITICUS	JOB	AMOS
NUMBERS	PSALMS	OBADIAH
DEUTERONOMY	PROVERBS	JONAH
JOSHUA	ECCLESIASTES	MICAH
JUDGES	SONG OF SONGS	NAHUM
RUTH	ISAIAH	HABAKKUK
SAMUEL	JEREMIAH	ZEPHANIAH
KINGS	LAMENTATIONS	HAGGAI
CHRONICLES	EZEKIEL	ZECHARIAH
EZRA	DANIEL	MALACHI

God Creates the First Man and Woman

Genesis 1:27

The most wonderful moment of creation came when God created Adam and Eve and placed them in a beautiful garden.

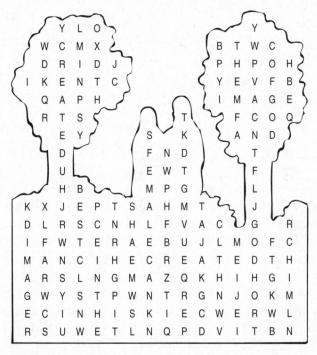

GOD	OWN	OF GOD	AND
CREATED	IMAGE	HE CREATED	FEMALE
MAN	IN THE	HIM	HE CREATED
IN HIS	IMAGE	MALE	THEM

Genesis 1:27 _____

_____

Adam and Eve Disobey God

Genesis 3

God gave Adam and Eve a wonderful place to live—the Garden of Eden. But He gave them one warning: "Do not eat the fruit on the tree of the knowledge of good and evil." Adam and Eve did not listen to God, and they ate the fruit. So God sent them out of the garden.

Can you start at the tree root and find your way to the fruit Eve is about to pick?

START

Noah Builds an Ark

Genesis 6–7

Do you see the little mouse next to Noah? Help the mouse find his way through the maze to his friend at the top of the ark.

The First Rainbow

Genesis 9

Can you find your way through the rainbow to the ark?
When you are done, color the rainbow.

The Tower of Babel

Genesis 11

Can you find your way to the top of the Tower of Babel and then back down to the bottom again?

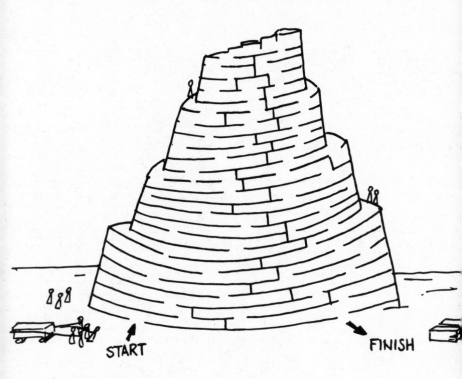

START

FINISH

God's Promise to Abraham

Genesis 12:2

Use the code key to figure out which letters should go on the blank lines below. For example, in this secret code, the number 4 represents the letter "A."

12		26 12 15 15		16 4 14 8		2 18 24

12 17 23 18		4		10 21 8 4 23

17 4 23 12 18 17 ,		4 17 7		12		26 12 15 15

5 15 8 22 22		2 18 24 ;		12		26 12 15 15

16 4 14 8		2 18 24 21		17 4 16 8		10 21 8 4 23

Code key:

A	B	C	D	E	F	G	H	I	J	K	L	M
4	5	6	7	8	9	10	11	12	13	14	15	16

N	O	P	Q	R	S	T	U	V	W	X	Y	Z
17	18	19	20	21	22	23	24	25	26	1	2	3

Genesis 12:2 _____

_____

_____

Abraham and Sarah Have a Son

Genesis 12; 18; 21

Abraham and Sarah lived in a place called Ur. One day God told Abraham, "I am going to give you many children, and they will become a great nation. I want you to go to a new land where your people will live someday."

Abraham and Sarah left their home and traveled to the new land. Many years went by, but they had no children. Again God told Abraham, "I will give you a son."

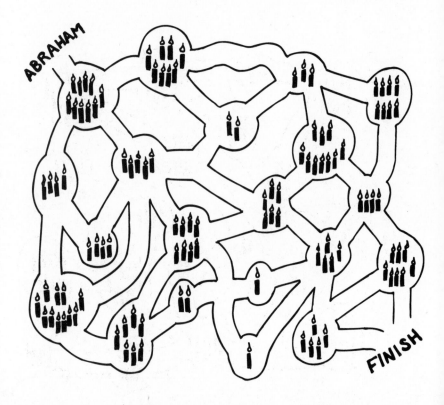

But more years went by, and still they had no son. They became very old and began to think it was impossible for them to have a child.

Finally, when Abraham was 100 years old and Sarah was 90, God gave them a son. They named him Isaac and were very happy because God had kept His promise!

There are two mazes on these pages—one for Abraham and one for Sarah. Can you figure out how to go through Abraham's maze and gather exactly 100 birthday candles? Now go through Sarah's maze and gather exactly 90 birthday candles.

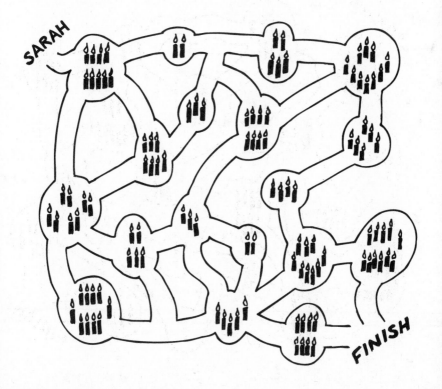

Great Bible Jokes and Riddles #1

1. Who was the fastest runner in the world?

2. How do we know that David was older than Goliath?

3. Who was the straightest man in the Bible?

4. Which man in the Bible had no parents?

5. Why was Moses the most wicked man who ever lived?

6. When is medicine first mentioned in the Bible?

7. Where did Noah strike the first nail on the ark?

8. What instructions did Noah give his sons about fishing off the ark?

9. Who was the most popular actor in the Bible?

10. What are the two strongest days of the week?

Twins Esau and Jacob

Genesis 25:24–27:40

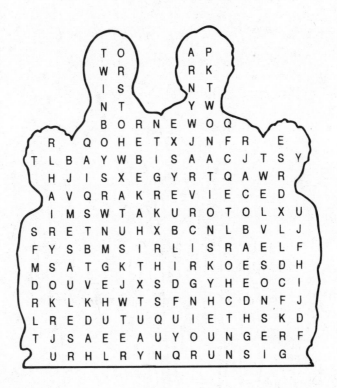

BIRTHRIGHT
BORN
DECEIVER
ESAU
HEEL
HAIRY
HUNTER

ISAAC
ISRAEL
JACOB
OLDER
QUIET
REBEKAH
RED

STEW
TWELVE SONS
TWIN BOYS
TWO NATIONS
YOUNGER

Joseph's Coat of Many Colors
Genesis 37

Jacob had 12 sons. Joseph was his favorite, and he gave him a beautiful coat of many colors. Can you find your way through Joseph's colored coat?

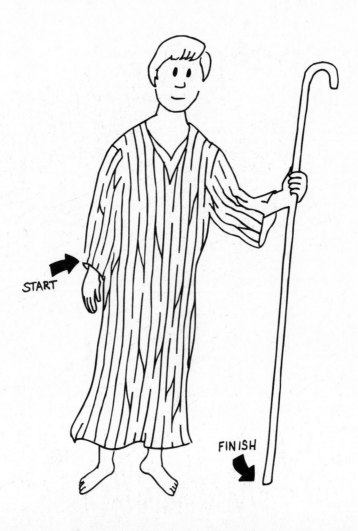

START

FINISH

The Baby in a Basket
Exodus 1:1–2:10

Pharaoh's daughter went to the river and saw a baby in a basket. He was crying, and she picked him up. Starting from the arrow at the bottom, can you find your way to Moses' basket?

The Ten Plagues
Exodus 5–12

In one of the plagues, God sent frogs all over Egypt. Can you find your way through the frogs?

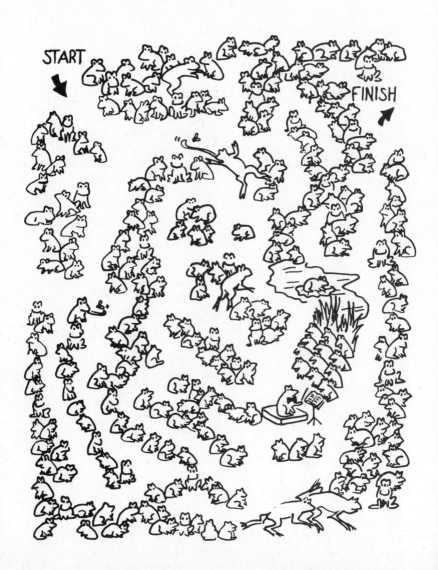

The Miracle at the Red Sea
Exodus 12:31–15:21

Can you find your way to the priests who are carrying the
Ark of the Covenant at the front of the crowd?

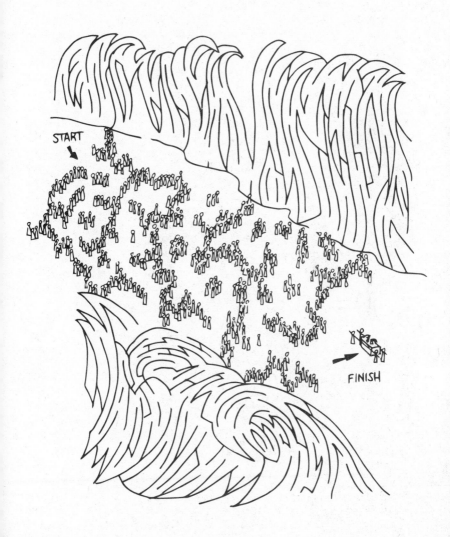

Wandering in the Wilderness

Numbers 15–34

Can you help the people of Israel find their way through the wilderness to the edge of the Promised Land?

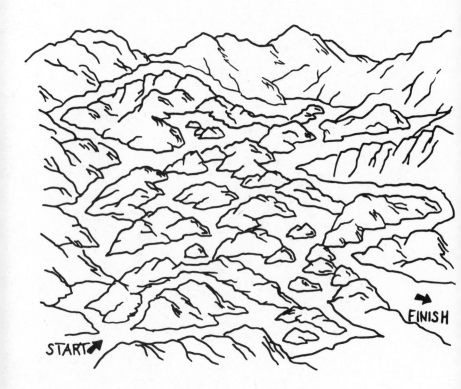

The Promised Land
Numbers 13–14

When the Israelites arrived at the edge of the Promised Land, God told Moses, "Send some men to explore the land." The cluster of grapes that the explorers brought back was large. Can you find your way through the cluster?

Marching Around Jericho
Joshua 1–6

God promised to give the people of Israel a new land. To enter it, they had to conquer the city of Jericho. God told the people to march around Jericho one time each day for six days. Then on the seventh day, they were to march around the city seven times, blow their trumpets, and shout. That's when the walls came tumbling down.

Can you help the Israelites find their way around Jericho and get to the front gates?

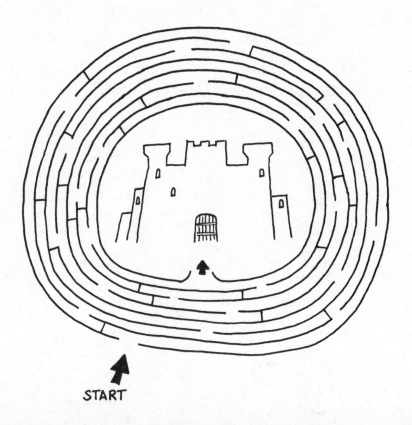

START

Fun with Numbers #1

1. In how many days did God create the world?

2. How many days and nights did it rain during the flood?

3. How many tribes were in the nation of Israel?

4. How many days was Jesus in the wilderness when Satan tempted Him?

5. How many copper coins (mites) did the poor widow put in the Temple treasury box?

6. How many spies did Moses send to explore the Promised Land?

7. How many years did the Israelites wander in the wilderness?

8. How many times did the Israelites march around Jericho on the day the walls fell?

9. How many disciples did Jesus choose?

10. How many years did it take for Noah to build the ark?

The Twelve Tribes of Israel

Joshua

Use the code key to figure out which letters should go on the blank lines below. For example, in this secret code, the number 9 represents a letter "A."

___ ___ ___ ___ ___
9   1   16   13   26

___ ___ ___
12   9   22

___ ___ ___ ___ ___ ___ ___ ___
17   1   1   9   11   16   9   26

___ ___ ___ ___ ___ ___
18   23   1   13   24   16

___ ___ ___ ___ ___ ___ ___ ___
22   9   24   2   16   9   20   17

___ ___ ___ ___ ___ ___
1   17   21   13   23   22

___ ___ ___ ___ ___ ___ ___ ___
10   13   22   18   9   21   17   22

___ ___ ___
15   9   12

___ ___ ___ ___ ___
18   3   12   9   16

___ ___ ___ ___
20   13   4   17

___ ___ ___ ___ ___ ___
26   13   3   10   13   22

___ ___ ___ ___ ___ ___ ___
8   13   10   3   20   3   22

Code key:

A	B	C	D	E	F	G	H	I	J	K	L	M
9	10	11	12	13	14	15	16	17	18	19	20	21

N	O	P	Q	R	S	T	U	V	W	X	Y	Z
22	23	24	25	26	1	2	3	4	5	6	7	8

The Key to True Success
Joshua 1:8

Did you know that when you put God first in your life, He will take care of everything for you? A great way to keep Him first in your life is to think about His Book (the Bible) every day and night.

DO NOT	FROM	YOU	YOU
LET	YOUR	MAY BE	WILL BE
THIS	MOUTH	CAREFUL	PROSPEROUS
BOOK	MEDITATE	TO DO	AND
OF THE	ON IT	EVERYTHING	SUCCESSFUL
LAW	DAY AND NIGHT	WRITTEN IN IT	
DEPART	SO THAT	THEN	

Joshua 1:8 _____

Samson, the Strongest Man in Israel

Judges 13–16

When Samson was born, God told his parents, "Samson must never cut his hair, or he will lose his strength." Can you find your way through Samson's hair?

The Story of Ruth

```
U  N  D  J  E  H  A  J  O  B  H  W  G  R  O  X  Q
J  A  R  A  M  B  D  P  W  T  M  I  H  P  S  O  N
M  O  S  W  U  O  N  I  U  K  H  R  M  O  A  B  R
R  M  T  L  A  G  W  R  P  L  R  K  T  W  N  M  J
S  I  O  R  P  A  H  E  N  K  F  I  E  L  D  S  I
F  Y  W  K  G  K  J  T  C  W  A  N  I  M  A  R  W
L  R  N  I  S  N  P  U  E  Y  P  S  Q  H  L  S  B
N  R  G  D  L  M  E  R  S  R  R  M  K  I  A  E  N
E  A  A  P  S  L  P  N  J  L  I  A  F  B  T  R  S
S  M  T  H  U  F  G  T  H  O  W  N  M  H  S  V  I
I  J  E  W  P  E  R  O  R  B  A  R  L  E  Y  A  R
B  Q  L  H  T  C  N  I  L  E  K  E  G  A  R  N  B
W  S  H  E  A  V  E  S  N  D  H  D  R  P  W  T  D
O  G  N  A  L  R  W  R  B  E  O  E  S  U  Y  G  L
C  A  J  T  G  K  V  A  M  W  K  E  G  R  A  I  N
E  W  S  I  E  L  D  E  R  S  Y  M  A  L  K  R  P
R  B  O  A  Z  R  Y  L  S  G  L  E  A  N  Q  L  G
P  M  J  W  Y  Q  U  B  I  T  A  R  H  E  K  S  D
```

BARLEY	HARVEST	RETURN TO ISRAEL
BETHLEHEM	I WILL GO	RUTH
BOAZ	KINSMAN REDEEMER	SANDAL
DAUGHTER IN LAW	MARRY	SERVANT GIRLS
ELDERS	MOAB	SHEAVES
FIELDS	NAOMI	SON
GLEAN	OBED	TOWN GATE
GRAIN	ORPAH	WHEAT

Hannah Gives Her Child to God
1 Samuel 1:1–2:11

Hannah was sad because she had no children. One day she prayed, "Lord, please give me a son, and I will give him back to You to serve You all the days of his life." Can you find your way through the maze?

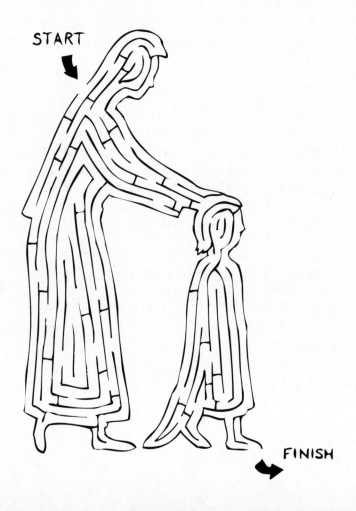

START

FINISH

Job—Faithful to God

Job

Long ago there was a man named Job who loved God very much. One day he lost all his animals and his children. Job's friends thought maybe he had done something wrong and God was punishing him. But Job had done nothing wrong. Even when he was suffering, he continued to trust God and stay faithful to Him.

Can you find the 30 times the name Job appears in the word search?

```
J A J C D N J Q G C Y J N I S Z T A
I O O W R U O E J O B V O A M C J C
V Y B K M L B R A H Z G F B T K O Y
D O N Z W R T U L N J O B X C F B W
J Q V A J O B G H D O Q P T N O C G
K H C U W H U Y T K B F N V J W Z A
P G F J A I W Z M Q U L K F A O Y C
T Z C O M A V E J U J O B R W H B I
J D Q B Y N T H O P N T X C F E G L
R O S T L E J O B G M B D J P J O B
H W B Y V W Z M L P O U T O D C K L
P Y E S J B F W E J I D H B F Z M W
J O B Y R W J S C B O M Y H J O B G
D S A L M J O B P U Y B E Q V A T S
R J Y T E Q B M R S T L N E C D P R
K O D J C A Z W T M C Y S R M J K T
C B K X O P K C J O B M C K D Q O L
F R N Q M B Y V P Z N Q J O B N E B
```

Saul—Israel's First King

1 Samuel 8–10

Saul was chosen to be the first king who ruled over the nation of Israel. Can you find your way through Saul's crown?

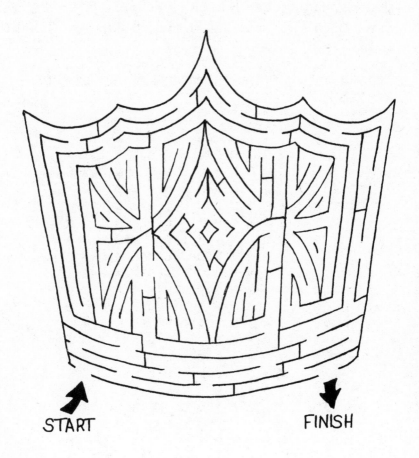

START   FINISH

God Is Worthy of Our Worship
1 Chronicles 16:25

The Bible tells us that God is great. He knows everything, is all-powerful, and is perfect. That's why we should worship Him. To worship God means saying good things about Him and obeying Him.

See if you can unscramble the letters of the words below.

```
  ___ ___ ___ ___ ___        ___ ___
   E   T   R   G   A          S   I

___ ___ ___      ___ ___ ___ ___      ___ ___
 E   T   H        O   D   R   L        N   D   A

___ ___ ___ ___      ___ ___ ___ ___ ___
 S   M   T   O        T   O   H   Y   W   R

    ___ ___      ___ ___ ___ ___ ___ ___
     F   O        I   A   R   E   P   S

___ ___      ___ ___      ___ ___      ___ ___
 E   H        S   I        O   T        E   B

___ ___ ___ ___ ___      ___ ___ ___ ___ ___
 R   F   D   E   A        V   O   A   B   E

    ___ ___ ___      ___ ___ ___ ___
     L   A   L        D   G   S   O
```

1 Chronicles 16:25 _____

_____

Which Came First? #1

1. The book of Job or the book of John?

2. Queen Vashti or Queen Esther?

3. Jesus feeding the 5,000 people or Jesus turning water into wine?

4. King Saul or King Solomon?

5. Jacob or Esau?

6. Jesus' arrest or Peter's denying Jesus three times?

7. The wise men or the shepherds?

8. Cain or Abel?

9. The Pharisees or the Philistines?

10. Moses or Noah?

Songs to the Lord

Psalms

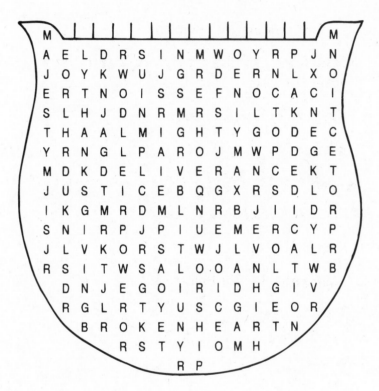

M															M
A	E	L	D	R	S	I	N	M	W	O	Y	R	P	J	N
J	O	Y	K	W	U	J	G	R	D	E	R	N	L	X	O
E	R	T	N	O	I	S	S	E	F	N	O	C	A	C	I
S	L	H	J	D	N	R	M	R	S	I	L	T	K	N	T
T	H	A	A	L	M	I	G	H	T	Y	G	O	D	E	C
Y	R	N	G	L	P	A	R	O	J	M	W	P	D	G	E
M	D	K	D	E	L	I	V	E	R	A	N	C	E	K	T
J	U	S	T	I	C	E	B	Q	G	X	R	S	D	L	O
I	K	G	M	R	D	M	L	N	R	B	J	I	I	D	R
S	N	I	R	P	J	P	I	U	E	M	E	R	C	Y	P
J	L	V	K	O	R	S	T	W	J	L	V	O	A	L	R
R	S	I	T	W	S	A	L	O	O	A	N	L	T	W	B
	D	N	J	E	G	O	I	R	I	D	H	G	I	V	
	R	G	L	R	T	Y	U	S	C	G	I	E	O	R	
	B	R	O	K	E	N	H	E	A	R	T	N			
	R	S	T	Y	I	O	M	H							
	R	P													

ALMIGHTY GOD	GLORY	POWER
BLESSING	HALLELUJAH	PROTECTION
BROKEN HEART	JOY	REJOICE
CONFESSION	JUSTICE	THANKSGIVING
DEDICATION	MAJESTY	WORSHIP
DELIVERANCE	MERCY	
DEVOTION	PRAISE	

The Lord Is My Shepherd
Psalm 23

Can you help the sheep in the lower left corner find its way to the shepherd?

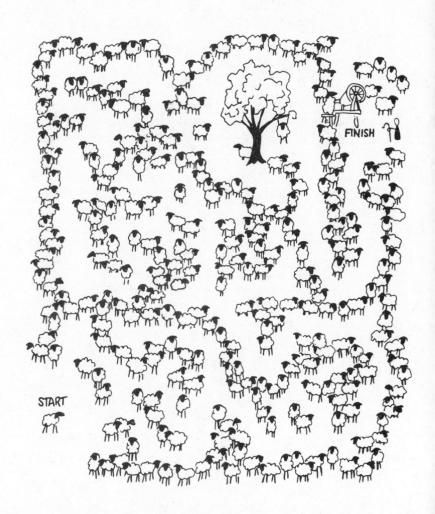

He Protects You

Psalm 121:7

God is able to watch over you and take care of you at all times. He is your great protector!

Can you figure out where each of the words in Psalm 121:7 should fit in the crossword puzzle? Three letters have already been provided to help you get started.

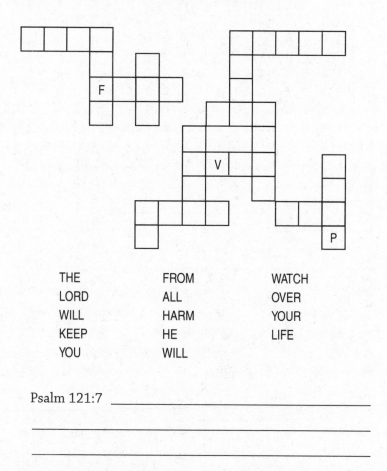

THE	FROM	WATCH
LORD	ALL	OVER
WILL	HARM	YOUR
KEEP	HE	LIFE
YOU	WILL	

Psalm 121:7 _____

_____

_____

The Coming Messiah

Isaiah 7:14; 9:6-7

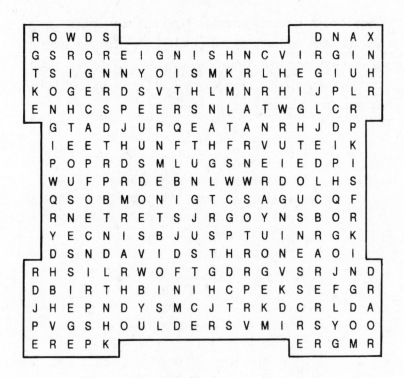

```
R O W D S                       D N A X
G S R O R E I G N I S H N C V I R G I N
T S I G N N Y O I S M K R L H E G I U H
K O G E R D S V T H L M N R H I J P L R
E N H C S P E E R S N L A T W G L C R
  G T A D J U R Q E A T A N R H J D P
  I E E T H U N F T H F R V U T E I K
  P O P R D S M L U G S N E I E D P I
  W U F P R D E B N L W W R D O L H S
  Q S O B M O N I G T C S A G U C Q F
  R N E T R E T S J R G O Y N S B O R
  Y E C N I S B J U S P T U I N R G K
  D S N D A V I D S T H R O N E A O I
R H S I L R W O F T G D R G V S R J N D
D B I R T H B I N I H C P E K S E F G R
J H E P N D Y S M C J T R K D C R L D A
P V G S H O U L D E R S V M I R S Y O O
E R E P K                       E R G M R
```

BIRTH	IMMANUEL	RIGHTEOUSNESS
CHILD	JUSTICE	SHOULDER
DAVID'S THRONE	KINGDOM	SIGN
EVERLASTING FATHER	MIGHTY GOD	SON
FOREVER	PRINCE OF PEACE	VIRGIN
GOVERNMENT	REIGN	WONDERFUL COUNSELOR

God's Great Love

Lamentations 3:22-23

The prophet Jeremiah wrote, "The Lord's love never ends. His mercies never stop. They are new every morning" (ICB). God's love for you never runs out—isn't that amazing? The words in Lamentations 3:22-23 are hidden in the word search puzzle. Can you find them?

```
M R S B D M T B N R S L T E
D O C A R G H I S Q D H R V
G L R U Z M E L R E M C A E
Q D H N O C G D C N E V E R
A M C X I P W A Q D Z S O Y
R G R B L N L U C S M R L A
E L M H F C G A B F T G B S
M Q E L R T L N E L O V E W
L O R D S G X D S U G H C B
D T C M U N B R M C S T O P
P R I C P D E C Z H R H X D
R Z E G C B H V G L D E G H
D G S L M R G D E X P Y C U
M C B A N E W O C R H W L R
```

THE	HIS	THEY
LORD'S	MERCIES	ARE
LOVE	NEVER	NEW
NEVER	STOP	EVERY
ENDS		MORNING

Prophets in the Old Testament

```
S   R   H   A   N   O   J   D   K   N   R   H
K   O   A   J   I   M   P   A   M   G   B   O
A   S   B   K   E   L   G   N   Z   H   L   S
J   G   A   A   M   L   E   I   K   E   Z   E
O   B   K   L   D   K   N   E   P   M   A   A
E   C   K   H   J   I   V   L   X   S   C   T
L   W   U   P   Q   M   A   L   A   C   H   I
C   H   K   J   K   D   S   H   P   D   A   F
H   A   G   G   A   I   A   T   L   I   R   O
B   K   K   N   D   I   U   O   B   S   I   H
N   A   H   U   M   Y   K   L   M   D   A   W
M   C   Z   E   P   H   A   N   I   A   H   S
V   G   R   L   A   E   G   P   C   B   G   O
K   E   Q   A   M   R   N   L   A   R   D   M
J   P   W   I   S   A   I   A   H   Y   C   A
```

AMOS	HOSEA	MALACHI
DANIEL	ISAIAH	MICAH
EZEKIEL	JEREMIAH	NAHUM
HABAKKUK	JOEL	OBADIAH
HAGGAI	JONAH	ZACHARIAH
		ZEPHANIAH

Daniel in the Lions' Den

Daniel 6

When Daniel prayed to God, his enemies became upset and had him thrown into the lions' den. God sent an angel to protect Daniel because he had done nothing wrong. Can you find your way through the maze in the lion's mane?

Daniel's Three Friends in the Furnace

Daniel 3

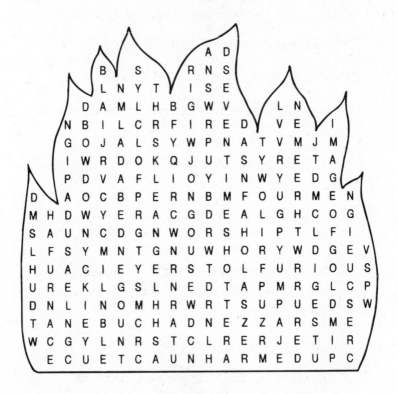

ABEDNEGO
ALL KINDS OF MUSIC
ANGEL
BIND
BOW DOWN
FIRE
FOUR MEN

FURIOUS
FURNACE
IMAGE OF GOLD
MESHACH
NEBUCHADNEZZAR
RESCUE
SEVEN TIMES HOTTER

SHADRACH
THREE MEN
UNHARMED
WALKING AROUND
WORSHIP

Great Bible Jokes and Riddles #2

1. Where is tennis mentioned in the Bible?

2. What animal took the most baggage onto the ark?

3. Where is baseball mentioned in the Bible?

4. Why didn't they play cards on Noah's ark?

5. What are two of the smallest insects mentioned in the Bible?

6. Where is the first math problem mentioned in the Bible?

7. Where does it talk about Honda automobiles in the Bible?

8. Methuselah was the oldest man in the Bible (969 years old), but he died before his father. How did that happen?

9. Was there any money on Noah's ark?

10. What city in the Bible has the same name as something you can find on every car?

Jonah and the Great Fish
Jonah

God told Jonah to go to the city of Nineveh and warn them that He would send judgment if they did not turn away from their sins. Jonah did not want to go and tried to run away from God by taking a ship in the opposite direction. When a bad storm came, the sailors on the ship threw Jonah overboard. A great fish swallowed him. Then Jonah prayed and asked God to help him. When the fish spit Jonah out on dry land, Jonah went to Nineveh just like God asked him to.

Can you find your way to Jonah inside the belly of the great fish?

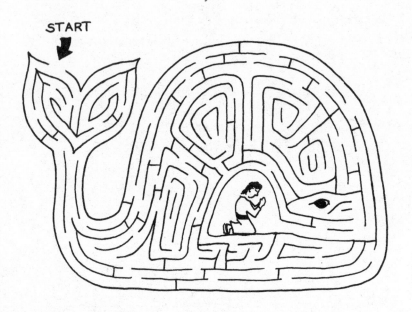

START

God's Great Care for You
Nahum 1:7

God can take care of you in both good times and bad. We might not understand why some things go wrong in our life, but we can know God is our refuge. The word refuge means "a place of protection."

Unscramble the letters below and write out the words to Nahum 1:7.

___ ___ ___   ___ ___ ___ ___   ___ ___
E   T   H   D   L   R   O   S   I

___ ___ ___ ___   ___   ___ ___ ___ ___ ___
O   D   O   G   A   F   E   R   G   E   U

___ ___   ___ ___ ___ ___ ___   ___ ___
N   I   E   M   S   T   I   F   O

___ ___ ___ ___ ___ ___   ___ ___
O   B   T   L   R   E   U   E   H

___ ___ ___ ___ ___   ___ ___ ___
A   R   S   C   E   O   R   F

___ ___ ___ ___ ___   ___ ___ ___
O   T   S   E   H   O   W   H

___ ___ ___ ___ ___   ___ ___   ___ ___ ___
S   T   R   U   T   N   I   M   H   I

Nahum 1:7 _____

_____

_____

The New Testament

```
T H W R T B R G M     O M J M P E T E R
E P H E S I A N S G S W B A Z D Y N M I E L
O H L E B T E J C R P J S T A L O G P Y V A
C I J V S U H A B U H V I T G B D J U D E G
H L O R G S I C O R I N T H I A N S M A L B
C E F L U D A O M S L K I E E L G J D O A T
J M A R K I E L D A I E L W O B Q U I S T I
K O B S R M T O O Q P R X Y S J R S E L I M
I N H Y L U Q S I N P A E T J X O E O N O O
T U B N L E O S D J I W C O N J M R W H N T
J I G F K O S I L E A A H E D I A N L S A H
P Q U U Y G D A H O N T N H E F N M I S R Y
G A L A T I A N S M S Y R S O J S Q E R D L
E P I S T L E S O F J O H N G U E V I S J L
```

MATTHEW	GALATIANS	PHILEMON
MARK	EPHESIANS	HEBREWS
LUKE	PHILIPPIANS	JAMES
JOHN	COLOSSIANS	PETER
ACTS	THESSALONIANS	EPISTLES OF JOHN
ROMANS	TIMOTHY	JUDE
CORINTHIANS	TITUS	REVELATION

Good News of Great Joy
Luke 2:8-15

On the night Jesus was born, some angels appeared to shepherds near Bethlehem to announce the birth of the Savior. The shepherds then went to see the new child.

Can you find your way through the maze?

The Birth of Jesus

Matthew 2:1-12; Luke 2:1-20

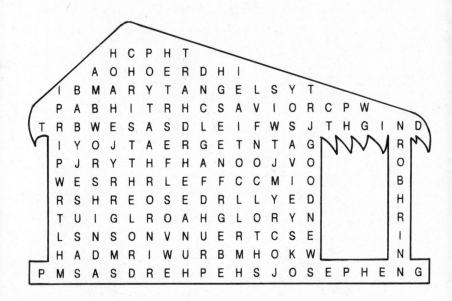

ANGELS

BABY JESUS

BETHLEHEM

BORN

CHRIST THE LORD

CLOTH

FIELD

FLOCKS

GLORY

GOOD NEWS

GREAT JOY

INN

JOSEPH

MANGER

MARY

NIGHT

PEACE TO MEN

SAVIOR

SHEPHERDS

TOWN OF DAVID

Baby Jesus
Luke 2:16-20

Can you find your way to the baby Jesus?

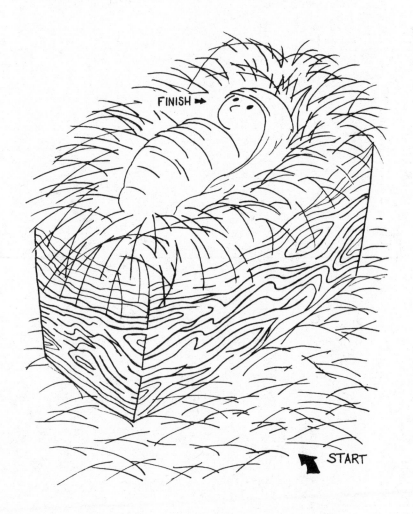

Jesus and John the Baptist
Matthew 3:1-17

Starting at Jesus, can you find your way through the river to John the Baptist?

The Twelve Disciples

Matthew 10:2-4

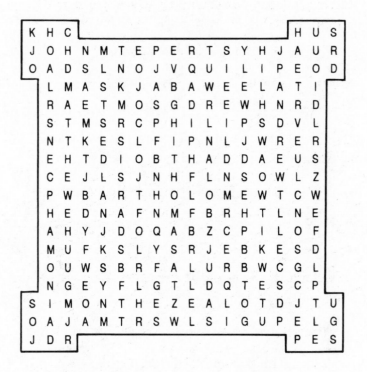

```
K H C                       H U S
J O H N M T E P E R T S Y H J A U R
O A D S L N O J V Q U I L I P E O D
  L M A S K J A B A W E E L A T I
  R A E T M O S G D R E W H N R D
  S T M S R C P H I L I P S D V L
  N T K E S L F I P N L J W R E R
  E H T D I O B T H A D D A E U S
  C E J L S J N H F L N S O W L Z
  P W B A R T H O L O M E W T C W
  H E D N A F N M F B R H T L N E
  A H Y J D O Q A B Z C P I L O F
  M U F K S L Y S R J E B K E S D
  O U W S B R F A L U R B W C G L
  N G E Y F L G T L D Q T E S C P
S I M O N T H E Z E A L O T D J T U
O A J A M T R S W L S I G U P E L G
J D R                       P E S
```

ANDREW	MATTHEW
BARTHOLOMEW	PETER
JAMES SON OF ALPHAEUS	PHILIP
JOHN SON OF ZEBEDEE	SIMON THE ZEALOT
JOHN	THADDAEUS
JUDAS	THOMAS

The Amazing Life of Jesus

1. Who baptized Jesus?

2. How many days did Jesus spend in the wilderness?

3. How many disciples did Jesus choose?

4. Which gate did Jesus say would take us to heaven—the wide gate or the narrow gate?

5. In Jesus' parable of the lost sheep, one sheep wandered away. How many were left?

6. What did Jesus say we should do to our enemies?

7. How many pieces of fish and bread did Jesus use to feed 5,000 people?

8. What is the name of the sea where Jesus walked on water?

9. Who climbed a tree so he could see Jesus better?

10. On what kind of animal did Jesus ride when He entered Jerusalem?

The Lamb of God
John 1:29

God sent Jesus to earth for a special reason: Jesus was to die on the cross to pay for the punishment we deserved for our sins. He came to take away our sin and make us righteous.

The verse below is written in secret code. Use the code key to figure out which letters to write above the numbers. For example, number 8 is the letter "A."

17	22	15	21	26	8	4	17	12	26	2	26

10	22	20	16	21	14	1	22	4	8	25	11

15 16 20   8 21 11   26 8 16 11

19 22 22 18   1 15 12   19 8 20 9

22 13   14 22 11   4 15 22

1 8 18 12 26   8 4 8 6

1 15 12   26 16 21   22 13

1 15 12   4 22 25 19 11

Code key:

A	B	C	D	E	F	G	H	I	J	K
8	9	10	11	12	13	14	15	16	17	18

L	M	N	O	P	Q	R	S	T	U	V
19	20	21	22	23	24	25	26	1	2	3

W	X	Y	Z
4	5	6	7

John 1:29 _____

_____

_____

The Gospel Message

John 3:16

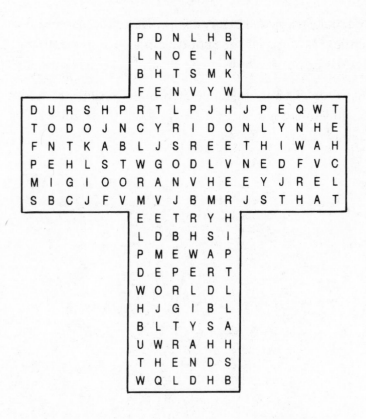

FOR	HIS	HIM
GOD	ONE	SHALL
SO	AND	NOT
LOVED	ONLY	PERISH
THE	SON	BUT
WORLD	THAT	HAVE
THAT	WHOEVER	ETERNAL
HE	BELIEVES	LIFE
GAVE	IN	

Fishers of Men

Mark 1:16-20

When Jesus picked the disciples, He said, "Come follow Me, and I will make you fishers of men."

What did Jesus mean when He said that? He planned to teach the disciples how to "catch" people and show them the way to heaven.

Can you find your way through the maze?

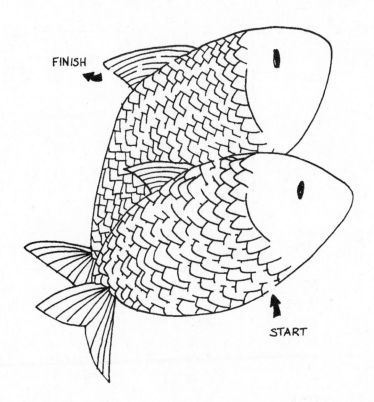

Jesus' Miracles

Can you figure out where to put each of Jesus' miracles into the crossword puzzle? Three letters have already been provided to help you get started.

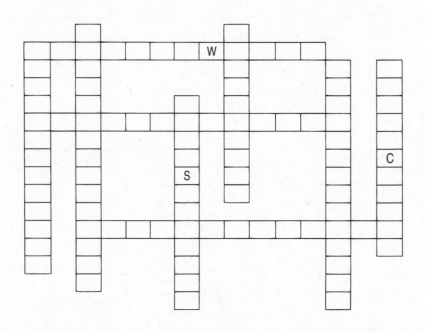

CALMS STORM	CASTS OUT DEMONS	CLEANSES LEPROSY
FEEDS CROWD	HEALS THE SICK	RAISES THE DEAD
RESTORES SIGHT	WALKS ON WATER	WATER INTO WINE

Jesus Feeds 5,000 People
Matthew 14:15-21

When Jesus fed 5,000 people, He used five loaves of bread and two fish. As you make your way through the maze, be sure to "visit" the five loaves and two fish.

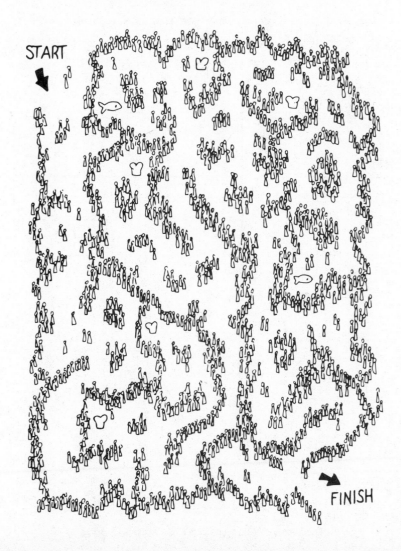

The Great Shepherd

John 10:27-28

A good shepherd watches his flock of sheep at all times to guide, feed, and protect them. Jesus is the Great Shepherd because He always helps us.

Can you figure out where each of the words in John 10:27-28 should fit in the crossword puzzle? Three letters have already been provided to help you get started.

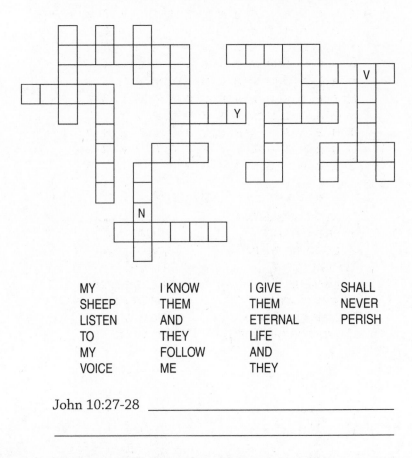

MY	I KNOW	I GIVE	SHALL
SHEEP	THEM	THEM	NEVER
LISTEN	AND	ETERNAL	PERISH
TO	THEY	LIFE	
MY	FOLLOW	AND	
VOICE	ME	THEY	

John 10:27-28 _____

_____

_____

Names of Jesus

Can you find all the names of Jesus in the word search puzzle?

```
T H E T R U T H R S T W L B Q J D
H S L N B R E A D O F L I F E K G
E Y Q D I F G W K Z R S G Y L I B
T I M M A N U E L P V Z H O U N D
R H G F I L C G R M D F T K X G C
U S O W U A P L J S O N O F G O D
E N O R S M T H S L E G F T W F Z
V G D N I B C N A W J F T E A K T
I A S C O O L S V A T L H N Y I H
N U H I Q F T Z I E N R E C A N E
E R E L N G M C O H A D W R H G W
M T P S R O L A R G C N O G L S O
R S H T L D W V N Z M D R M Y V R
T H E W A Y X R G C J U L I E N D
Q U R P T H E L I F E O D H K G C
J E D B Q S H I G H P R I E S T A
```

ALPHA AND OMEGA
BREAD OF LIFE
GOOD SHEPHERD
HIGH PRIEST
IMMANUEL
KING OF KINGS
LAMB OF GOD
LIGHT OF THE WORLD

SAVIOR
SON OF GOD
SON OF MAN
THE LIFE
THE TRUE VINE
THE TRUTH
THE WAY
THE WORD

Jesus Is the Only Way

John 14:6

How can you get to heaven? Jesus said there is only one way: by receiving Him as your Savior and Lord.

Solve this crossword puzzle and see what Jesus said about Himself in John 14:6. Three letters have already been provided to help you get started.

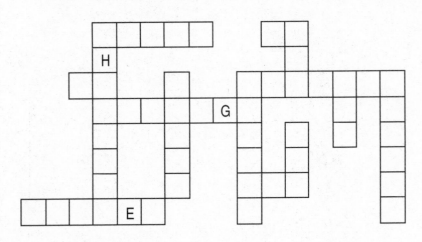

I AM	THE LIFE	FATHER
THE WAY	NO	EXCEPT
AND	ONE	THROUGH
THE TRUTH	COMES	ME
AND	TO THE	

John 14:6 _____

_____

_____

Parable of the Sower
Matthew 13:1-23

In the parable of the sower, Jesus said, "If a person's heart is hard, he will not receive my message of salvation. But a person with a soft heart will listen, grow, bear fruit, and do many great things for Me." Can you find your way from the "start" arrow to the farmer's hand?

Famous Men of the Bible

```
A  D  A  M  C  T  L  B  G  D  I  V  A  D
J  B  P  Z  D  I  M  O  S  E  S  L  C  A
Q  V  R  C  M  T  J  C  K  X  P  R  T  N
W  N  G  A  K  U  B  A  F  T  Y  G  K  I
L  I  Z  O  H  S  G  J  O  S  H  U  A  E
U  M  E  S  I  A  O  H  D  A  L  Y  M  L
A  O  C  N  Z  E  M  C  I  M  D  H  P  W
P  W  H  H  T  J  I  A  V  U  P  T  I  Y
L  D  A  J  V  O  H  A  H  E  D  O  U  L
M  O  R  T  Y  S  B  S  O  L  O  M  O  N
N  B  I  E  Z  E  K  I  E  L  F  I  E  R
X  U  A  D  V  P  R  Y  T  D  Z  T  E  S
J  O  H  N  T  H  E  B  A  P  T  I  S  T
```

ABRAHAM	JACOB	PAUL
ADAM	JOHN THE BAPTIST	SAMUEL
DANIEL	JOSEPH	SOLOMON
DAVID	JOSHUA	TIMOTHY
EZEKIEL	MOSES	TITUS
ISAAC	NOAH	ZECHARIAH

Famous Women of the Bible

```
E  V  E  J  M  A  I  R  I  M  D  Y  P  S
H  I  A  N  A  O  M  I  F  R  C  Y  A  D
M  R  S  B  R  D  L  D  E  B  O  R  A  H
Z  G  M  X  T  W  L  Z  R  M  A  N  N  A
P  I  F  S  H  A  E  S  T  H  E  R  M  H
V  N  L  E  A  H  R  G  N  R  T  V  I  T
O  M  F  L  N  B  E  R  H  A  H  D  L  E
M  A  R  Y  O  F  B  E  T  H  A  N  Y  B
E  R  Z  R  T  M  E  R  D  G  N  R  D  A
S  Y  A  H  D  C  K  O  M  L  N  H  I  Z
C  H  T  M  L  E  A  V  Q  K  A  C  A  I
T  U  E  S  R  A  H  A  B  Y  H  L  B  L
R  A  C  H  E  L  D  T  H  N  B  R  C  E
```

ANNA	LEAH	RACHEL
DEBORAH	LYDIA	RAHAB
ELIZABETH	MIRIAM	REBEKAH
ESTHER	MARTHA	RUTH
EVE	MARY OF BETHANY	SARAH
HANNAH	NAOMI	VIRGIN MARY

Jesus and the Disciples in the Storm
Matthew 8:18-27

Begin at the "start" arrow and find your way to Jesus, who is standing in the front of the boat.

START

The Prodigal Son
Luke 15:11-32

Can you help the wayward son find the right path home to his father?

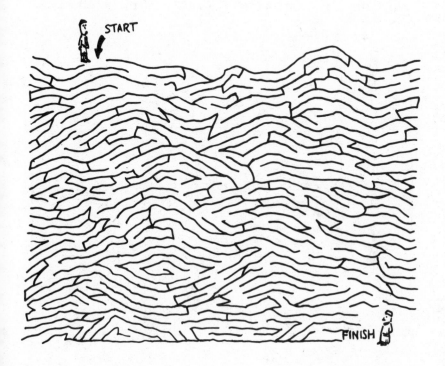

Zacchaeus in the Tree

Luke 19:2-10

One day Jesus came to visit the town where Zacchaeus lived. Zacchaeus was short and could not see above the crowd, so he climbed a tree. When Jesus walked by, He said, "Zacchaeus, come down. I need to stay at your house." After meeting Jesus, Zacchaeus became a much nicer person.

Can you find your way through the tree? Start near Zacchaeus and try to get down to the ground.

Plants of the Bible

Can you figure out where to put the plants of the Bible? Three letters have already been provided to help you get started.

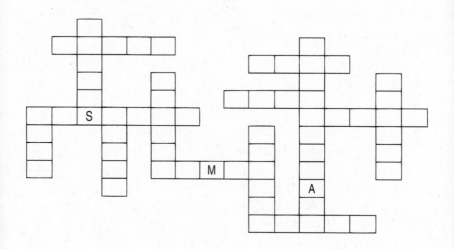

ALOE	LEEKS	TARES
BARLEY	LENTIL	THORNS
CUMIN	MINT	VINE
GARLIC	MUSTARD	WHEAT
GOURD	POMEGRANATE	

Jesus Enters Jerusalem on a Donkey

Matthew 21:1-11

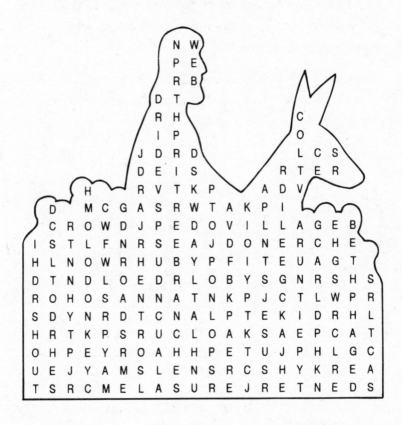

BETHPHAGE

CLOAKS

COLT

CROWD

DONKEY

ENTER JERUSALEM

HOSANNA

JESUS

MOUNT OF OLIVES

RIDE

ROAD

SHOUT

SON OF DAVID

TREE BRANCHES

TWO DISCIPLES

UNTIE

VILLAGE

Which Came First? #2

1. John the Baptist or Jesus?

2. Rachel or Rebekah?

3. The book of Ruth or the book of Esther?

4. Joseph or Joshua?

5. The flood or the Tower of Babel?

6. King David or the prophet Daniel?

7. Moses at the burning bush or Moses with the Ten Commandments?

8. Jesus being baptized or Jesus walking on water?

9. Adam or Abraham?

10. Jesus' baptism or the Lord's prayer?

The Holy Spirit Is Your Teacher
John 14:26

Can you figure out where each of the words in John 14:26 go in the crossword puzzle? Three letters have already been provided to help you get started.

THE	IN MY NAME	YOU
HOLY	WILL	OF
SPIRIT	TEACH	EVERYTHING
WHOM	YOU	I HAVE
THE	ALL THINGS	SAID
FATHER	AND	TO YOU
WILL	WILL	
SEND	REMIND	

John 14:26 _____

_____

_____

The Vine and the Branches
John 15:1-8

Jesus said, "I am the vine, and you are the branches. As long as you, the branch, stay connected to Me, the vine, you will bear fruit."

Can you find your way from the branch (you) to the vine (Jesus)?

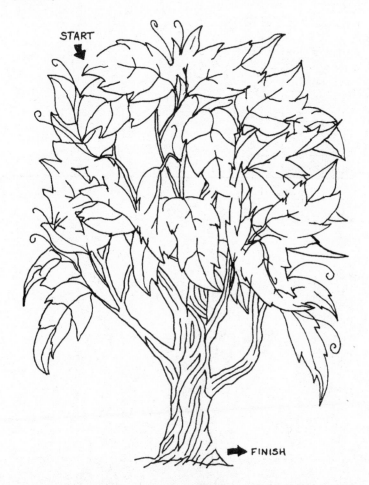

The Last Supper

Matthew 26:20-29; Mark 14:12-25;
Luke 22:7-23; John 13:1-17

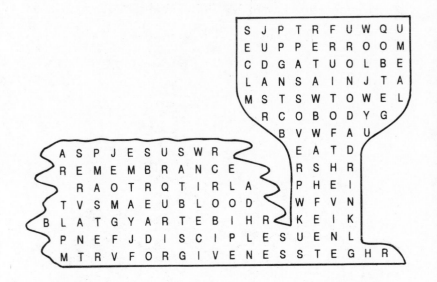

BETRAY	FORGIVENESS	REMEMBRANCE
BLOOD	FRUIT OF THE VINE	SERVANT
BODY	JESUS	TOWEL
BREAD	JUDAS	UPPER ROOM
CUP	MASTER	WASH FEET
DISCIPLES	MEAL	WATER
DRINK	PASSOVER	
EAT	PETER	

Jesus on the Cross
John 18–19

The day Jesus died on the cross was a sad day. But He conquered death and rose again three days later.

Can you find your way up the hill to the cross?

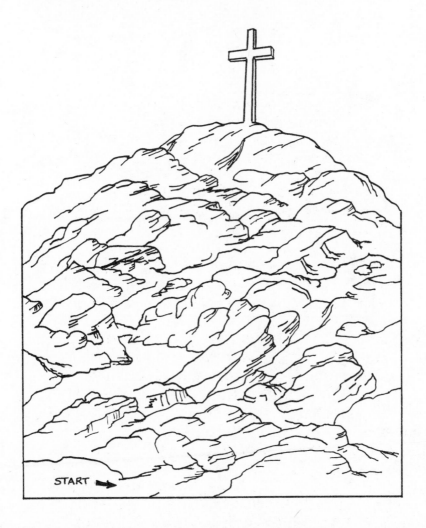

He Is Risen!

John 20:1-20

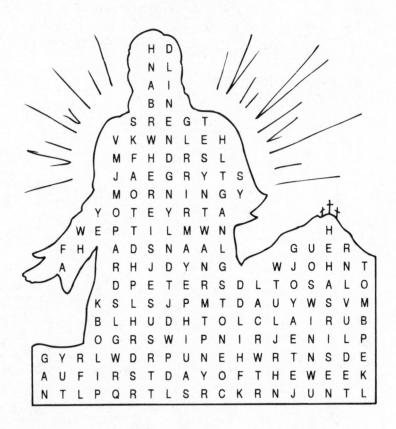

ANGELS
BURIAL CLOTH
FIRST DAY OF THE WEEK
HE HAS RISEN
JOHN
JOY

LINEN
MARY MAGDALENE
MORNING
PETER
ROLLED AWAY
RUN

STONE
TOMB
WEPT
WHERE IS JESUS

First and Last

1. Who was the first child born in the Bible?

2. What is the name of the first person who appears in the Bible?

3. Who was Israel's first king?

4. Who was the first mother?

5. What were Jesus' last words?

6. What is the first book in the Bible?

7. What is the first book of the New Testament?

8. What is the last book of the Bible?

9. What was the first plague in Egypt?

10. What was Jesus' first miracle?

Go Tell the World
Matthew 28:19-20

Before Jesus went up to heaven, He told the disciples, "Go tell everyone the good news that I am alive. Go tell the world what I have taught you and let everyone know how they can become saved."

Jesus also wants you to share with other people how they can become Christians. Can you find your way to the four different children of the world?

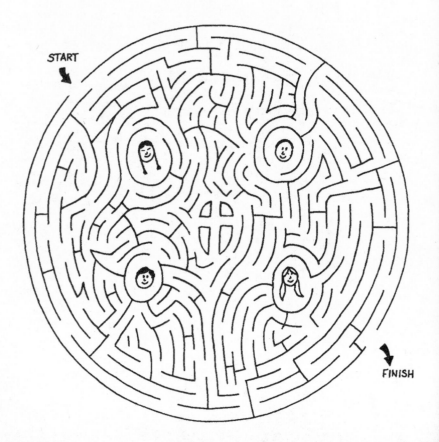

Paul's Journey to Rome

Acts 27–28

Can you help Paul's ship find its way to Rome?

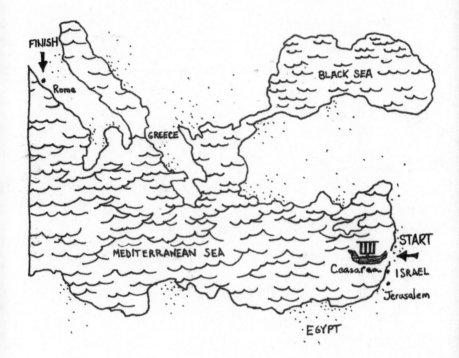

What's the Missing Word? #1

1. "Rejoice in the Lord _____."

2. "I can do everything through him who gives me _____."

3. "Search me, O God, and know my _____."

4. "In the beginning was the _____."

5. "Go into all the _____."

6. "Jesus Christ is the same _____ and today and forever."

7. "Children, _____ your parents in everything."

8. "You must be born _____."

9. "Love your _____ as yourself."

10. "Love the Lord your God with all your _____."

A Free Gift

Romans 6:23

Because of sin, no one can get to heaven. God is pure, and He cannot allow sin in heaven. But when Jesus died on the cross, He took the punishment for our sins. We can ask Him to forgive us, make our hearts clean, and give us the gift of eternal life. Then we can go to heaven!

The verse below is written in secret code. Use the code key to figure out which letters to write above the numbers. For example, number 13 is the letter "A."

___ ___ ___   ___ ___ ___ ___ ___   ___ ___   ___ ___ ___
6   20 17   9   13 19 17 5   1   18   5   21 26

  ___ ___   ___ ___ ___ ___ ___   ___ ___ ___
  21 5   16 17 13 6   20   14 7   6

    ___ ___ ___   ___ ___ ___ ___   ___ ___
    6   20 17   19 21 18 6   1   18

  ___ ___ ___   ___ ___   ___ ___ ___ ___ ___ ___ ___
  19 1   16   21 5   17 6   17 4   26 13 24

  ___ ___ ___ ___   ___ ___   ___ ___ ___ ___ ___ ___
  24 21 18 17   21 26   15 20 4   21 5   6

  ___ ___ ___ ___ ___   ___ ___ ___   ___ ___ ___ ___
  22 17 5   7   5   1   7   4   24 1   4   16

Code key:

A	B	C	D	E	F	G	H	I	J	K	L	M	N	O
13	14	15	16	17	18	19	20	21	22	23	24	25	26	1

P	Q	R	S	T	U	V	W	X	Y	Z
2	3	4	5	6	7	8	9	10	11	12

Romans 6:23 _____

_____

Confess and Believe

Romans 10:9

Romans 10:9 is a wonderful verse that explains how you can become a Christian. If you have a friend who wants to become a Christian, you can share this verse with him or her.

```
T  L  R  N                          S  J  D  R
D  C  A  K  A  R  D  B  E  L  I  E  V  E  C  F
R  W  I  L  L  B  E  K  A  M  C  Q  H  S  R  D
L  D  S  N  K  W  A  Y  N  G  O  D  A  U  T  E
K  R  E  H  Y  P  N  O  C  B  N  G  E  S  L  A
A  N  D  F  L  O  W  E  S  W  F  Y  D  I  N  D
   A  Q  R  E  R  U  J  T  H  E  P  W  S  E
   E  Y  O  U  S  D  R  M  U  S  T  N  L  T
D  L  O  M  N  T  P  L  H  J  S  L  Y  O  U  R
K  B  K  S  O  E  N  Y  V  E  U  M  L  R  A  I
W  I  T  H  L  U  J  B  O  W  A  C  T  D  C  F
S  G  H  N  R  S  T  A  J  P  B  R  S  L  P  Y
M  S  A  V  E  D  A  H  I  M  J  P  T  N  K  O
R  N  T  L                       H  U  W  U
```

IF YOU	BELIEVE	THE
CONFESS	IN YOUR HEART	DEAD
WITH	THAT	YOU
YOUR	GOD	WILL BE
MOUTH	RAISED	SAVED
JESUS IS LORD	HIM	
AND	FROM	

Romans 10:9 _____

_____

Your Heart, the Spirit's Home

1 Corinthians 6:19

When you receive Jesus as your Savior, your body becomes the home of the Holy Spirit. Because He lives in you, you want to be careful about how you live so that the Spirit isn't saddened or disappointed.

To put the following words in the right order, start at the beginning of each rope and follow it to the correct blank line.

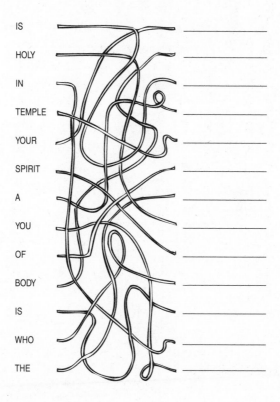

IS

HOLY

IN

TEMPLE

YOUR

SPIRIT

A

YOU

OF

BODY

IS

WHO

THE

1 Corinthians 6:19 _____

A Way Out of Temptation

1 Corinthians 10:13

Let's pretend that, by accident, you broke a pretty dish that belonged to your parents. They didn't see you do it. In your heart, you are tempted to tell a lie and say that you didn't break the dish. Will you tell the lie, or will you tell the truth and say it was your fault? Anytime you are thinking about doing something wrong, you are being tempted. But you don't have to choose the wrong way. God has given you the power to do what is right. He promises to make a way out of temptation. Will you choose God's way? Memorizing 1 Corinthians 10:13 will help you do that.

GOD	BE TEMPTED	BUT	ALSO
IS	BEYOND	WHEN	PROVIDE
FAITHFUL	WHAT	YOU ARE	A WAY OUT
HE WILL	YOU CAN	TEMPTED	
NOT LET YOU	BEAR	HE WILL	

1 Corinthians 10:13 _____

_____

Animals in the Bible

```
E  R  B  J  D  F  L  O  W  C  M  I  A  P
S  A  H  C  P  O  Q  G  H  O  T  D  N  R
T  K  G  X  L  X  E  B  A  A  H  G  T  E
W  O  R  L  B  M  B  H  L  I  O  N  R  C
J  H  V  M  E  W  A  O  E  V  R  T  P  A
L  N  P  K  E  H  D  F  H  C  S  F  H  W
D  T  F  L  S  G  L  R  N  T  E  L  U  M
T  O  W  I  C  I  O  X  T  B  P  S  G  H
B  L  G  O  A  T  C  P  G  E  R  H  X  F
F  U  H  A  U  D  U  H  Q  S  L  G  N  R
I  C  D  Y  G  P  S  E  U  J  H  B  Y  O
S  E  R  P  E  N  T  W  A  E  D  E  O  G
H  K  O  C  I  U  F  D  I  L  U  A  E  N
D  W  J  T  C  A  M  E  L  M  Q  R  A  P
```

ANT	FOX	OX
BEAR	FROG	QUAIL
BEES	GOAT	SERPENT
CAMEL	HORSE	SHEEP
DOG	LION	WHALE
EAGLE	LOCUST	WOLF
FISH	MULE	

Doing All to God's Glory

1 Corinthians 10:31

Can your family and friends tell that you love God by the way you think, talk, and act? What are some ways you can show your love for God at home, at school, with your family, and with your friends? When you do those things you will glorify God—you will be putting Him first in your life and other people will thank Him for what He is doing through you.

The verse below is written in secret code. Use the code key to figure out which letters to write above the numbers. For example, number 8 is the letter "A."

```
 4  15  12   1  15  12  25        6  22   2          12   8   1

      22  25      11  25  16  21  18        22  25

  4  15   8   1  12   3  12  25        6  22   2

     11  22      11  22      16   1        8  19  19

 13  22  25       1  15  12      14  19  22  25   6

               22  13      14  22  11
```

Code key:

A	B	C	D	E	F	G	H	I	J	K
8	9	10	11	12	13	14	15	16	17	18

L	M	N	O	P	Q	R	S	T	U	V
19	20	21	22	23	24	25	26	1	2	3

W	X	Y	Z
4	5	6	7

1 Corinthians 10:31 _____

_____

God's Kind of Love

1 Corinthians 13:4-8

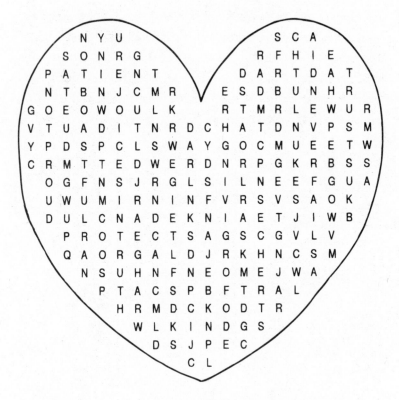

FORGIVING NOT BOASTFUL PATIENT
HOPES NOT ENVIOUS PERSEVERES
KIND NOT PROUD PROTECTS
NEVER FAILS NOT RUDE REJOICES IN TRUTH
NOT ANGRY NOT SELFISH TRUSTS

From Sin to Righteousness

2 Corinthians 5:21

When Jesus died on the cross, God did something very amazing. He gave our sin to Jesus, and gave Jesus' righteousness to us. That may be hard to understand, but that's exactly what happened. Aren't you thankful that Jesus was willing to go through so much pain so you could become righteous before God?

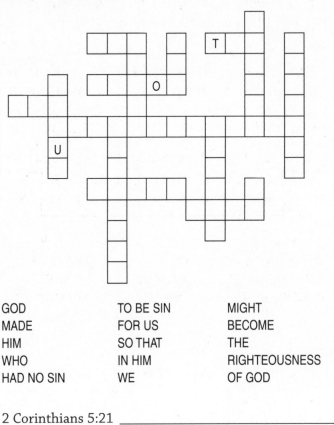

GOD	TO BE SIN	MIGHT
MADE	FOR US	BECOME
HIM	SO THAT	THE
WHO	IN HIM	RIGHTEOUSNESS
HAD NO SIN	WE	OF GOD

2 Corinthians 5:21 _____

_____

_____

The Fruit of the Spirit

Galatians 5:22-23

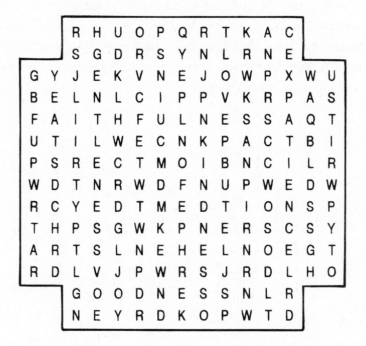

R	H	U	O	P	Q	R	T	K	A	C
	S	G	D	R	S	Y	N	L	R	N	E
G	Y	J	E	K	V	N	E	J	O	W	P	X	W	U
B	E	L	N	L	C	I	P	P	V	K	R	P	A	S
F	A	I	T	H	F	U	L	N	E	S	S	A	Q	T
U	T	I	L	W	E	C	N	K	P	A	C	T	B	I
P	S	R	E	C	T	M	O	I	B	N	C	I	L	R
W	D	T	N	R	W	D	F	N	U	P	W	E	D	W
R	C	Y	E	D	T	M	E	D	T	I	O	N	S	P
T	H	P	S	G	W	K	P	N	E	R	S	C	S	Y
A	R	T	S	L	N	E	H	E	L	N	O	E	G	T
R	D	L	V	J	P	W	R	S	J	R	D	L	H	O
	G	O	O	D	N	E	S	S	N	L	R
	N	E	Y	R	D	K	O	P	W	T	D

FAITHFULNESS	JOY	PATIENCE
GENTLENESS	KINDNESS	PEACE
GOODNESS	LOVE	SELF CONTROL

Saved by Grace Alone

Ephesians 2:8-9

The Bible teaches us that salvation is a free gift that God wants to give to us. It's because of His grace, or His goodness, that we are able to become saved. We can't go to heaven by being good on our own; only Jesus can change our hearts to become right and pure.

IT IS BY	AND	NOT
GRACE	THIS	BY WORKS
YOU	NOT	SO THAT
HAVE	FROM	NO ONE
BEEN	YOURSELVES	CAN
SAVED	IT IS THE	BOAST
THROUGH	GIFT	
FAITH	OF GOD	

Ephesians 2:8-9 _____

_____

_____

Great Bible Jokes and Riddles #3

1. When the ark landed on Mount Ararat, was Noah the first one out?

2. Matthew and Mark have two things not found in Luke and John. What are they?

3. Where did the Israelites deposit their money?

4. In the Bible, who introduced the first walking stick?

5. What do you have that Cain, Abel, and Seth never had?

6. What time was Adam born?

7. What story in the Bible tells about a very lazy boy?

8. How many of each animal did Moses take on the ark?

9. Why was Adam's first day the longest?

10. What does God give away and keep at the same time?

Loving Your Parents
Ephesians 6:1

Why does God want us to obey Him? Because He is wise and knows what is best for us. That is the same reason God wants us to obey our parents—they are wise and know what's best. When we obey them, we are showing that we love them.

To put the following words in the right order, start at the beginning of each rope and follow it to the correct blank line.

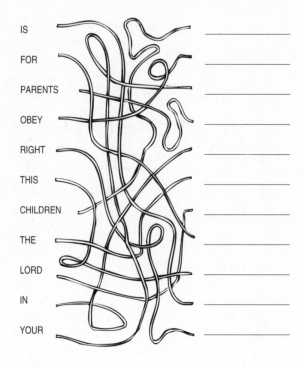

IS

FOR

PARENTS

OBEY

RIGHT

THIS

CHILDREN

THE

LORD

IN

YOUR

Ephesians 6:1 _____

_____

_____

Serving Other People First

Philippians 2:4

Have you ever played with a friend who wants to have all the fun and won't let you have fun too? Or eaten with someone who wants the biggest or best pieces of food for himself without thinking about others? What can you do to make sure you are not selfish? What are some ways you can serve other people before you serve yourself?

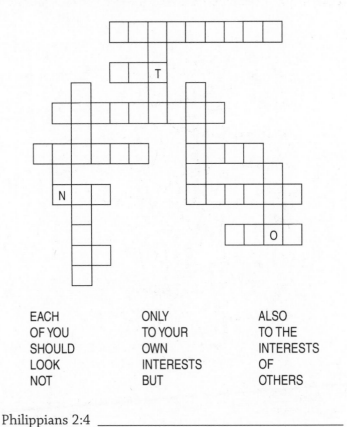

EACH	ONLY	ALSO
OF YOU	TO YOUR	TO THE
SHOULD	OWN	INTERESTS
LOOK	INTERESTS	OF
NOT	BUT	OTHERS

Philippians 2:4 _____

_____

Sharing Your Needs with God

Philippians 4:6

Are you worried about something? God wants you to share your worries with Him. When you do that, He can help replace your worry with peace.

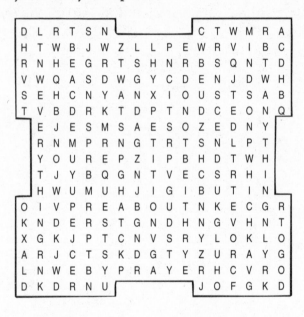

DO NOT BE
ANXIOUS
ABOUT
ANYTHING
BUT IN
EVERYTHING
BY PRAYER
AND

PETITION
WITH
THANKSGIVING
PRESENT
YOUR
REQUESTS
TO GOD

Philippians 4:6 _____

_____

_____

The Right Kinds of Thoughts

Philippians 4:8

What kinds of thoughts are in your mind today? Have you been angry at someone? Do you wish you could hurt someone back? Those kinds of thoughts make God sad. He wants us to think about what is true, right, pure, and anything else that is good.

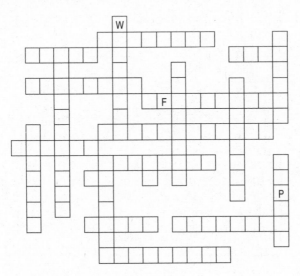

WHATEVER	IS PURE	EXCELLENT
IS TRUE	WHATEVER	OR
WHATEVER	IS LOVELY	PRAISEWORTHY
IS NOBLE	WHATEVER	THINK
WHATEVER	IS ADMIRABLE	ABOUT
IS RIGHT	IF ANYTHING	SUCH
WHATEVER	IS	THINGS

Philippians 4:8 _____

_____

_____

What's the Missing Word? #2

1. "Seek _____ his kingdom and his righteousness."

2. "The Lord is my _____, I shall not be in want."

3. "I am the _____ and the truth and the life."

4. "I am the resurrection and the _____."

5. "For it is by grace you have been saved, through _____."

6. "I have hidden your word in my _____."

7. "Your word is a _____ to my feet."

8. "You are the _____ of the world."

9. "For God so loved the _____ that he gave his one and only Son."

10. "Everyone who believes in him may have _____ life."

God's Word in Your Heart
Colossians 3:16

What is one way we can grow closer to God and become stronger in the Christian life? Memorize God's Word in our heart!

To memorize something means to repeat it in your mind again and again so that you'll never forget it. Colossians 3:16 says, "Let the word of Christ dwell in you richly."

Can you find your way through the Bible maze?

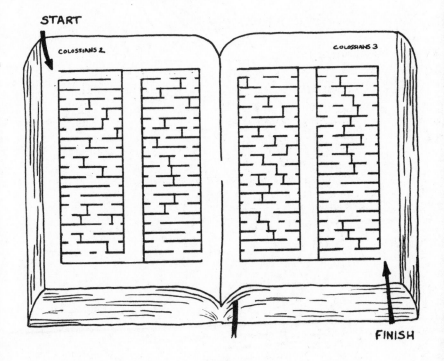

Praying and Giving Thanks

1 Thessalonians 5:17-18

First Thessalonians 5:17-18 says, "Pray continually; [and] give thanks in all circumstances." Do you pray to God each day and thank Him for His good gifts to you?

Can you find your way through the maze?

Our Guide to the Christian Life

2 Timothy 3:16

The Bible is an amazing book. In it God tells us how we can grow stronger and wiser. The Bible also helps us to see if we're doing anything wrong in our lives. In fact, the Bible tells us everything we need to know about living the Christian life!

ALL	IS USEFUL	CORRECTING
SCRIPTURE IS	FOR	AND
GOD BREATHED	TEACHING	TRAINING IN
AND	REBUKING	RIGHTEOUSNESS

2 Timothy 3:16 _____

_____

_____

A Double-Edged Sword

Hebrews 4:12

When we read the Bible, it helps us to know if our thoughts or attitudes are right or wrong. The Bible is like a sharp, two-edged sword that shows what is inside our hearts.

```
                                    R
        I D L C         K R S W
    T M R T N O F T H E L P E J Y S
    L H D P R M U E A C T I V E T W
    Y E A E T A H B W Y H R E L H O
    I A Q N H R I S L I V I N G O R
    T R A E E R N C J E R T T W U D
    J T N T I O F G O D E H O A G N
    U J D R J W T J I A N D T N H S
    D S H A R P E R N C O E G Y T O
    G W K T J G A T T I T U D E S U
    E T H E C W L N S M W O R D D L
    S R U S D I V I D I N G E A N D
```

THE	DOUBLE EDGED	AND
WORD	SWORD	MARROW
OF GOD	IT PENETRATES	IT JUDGES
IS LIVING	EVEN TO	THE
AND	DIVIDING	THOUGHTS
ACTIVE	SOUL	AND
SHARPER	AND	ATTITUDES
THAN	SPIRIT	OF THE
ANY	JOINTS	HEART

Hebrews 4:12_____

_____

_____

Fun with Numbers #2

1. How many people lived in the Garden of Eden?

2. How many years were the Jewish people kept captive in Babylon?

3. How many books are in the Bible?

4. How many sons did Jacob have?

5. How many days was Jonah in the stomach of the big fish?

6. How many plagues did God send upon Egypt?

7. How many thieves were crucified with Jesus?

8. How many times a day did Daniel pray?

9. How many people did Jesus feed with five loaves of bread and two fish?

10. How many pieces of silver were given to Judas for betraying Jesus?

Jesus Never Changes

Hebrews 13:8

Jesus will always love and care for us. He will always be perfectly wise and fair. We know this because of what Hebrews 13:8 says.

To put the words in this verse in the right order, start at the beginning of each rope and follow it to the correct blank line. Then write the correct words in the blanks.

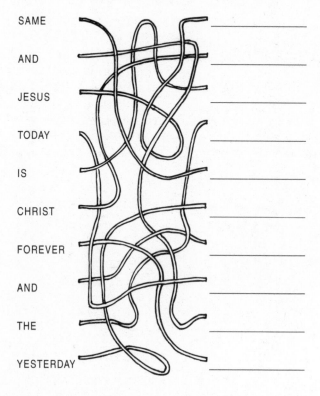

SAME   _____

AND   _____

JESUS   _____

TODAY   _____

IS   _____

CHRIST   _____

FOREVER   _____

AND   _____

THE   _____

YESTERDAY _____

Hebrews 13:8_____

_____

When You Need Wisdom

James 1:5

Every day we have questions that we're not sure how to answer. For example, what should we do when a friend asks us to do something wrong? What should we say when someone teases us? Sometimes we need help deciding how to use our time or money. Whenever we're not sure of what to do, we should ask God for wisdom. He will guide us to the right answer. We can trust His wisdom because He knows everything.

```
        A H T O H I M W C K W A
        N K Y R W S D B I E J R
  K V D R S L I N F E Z S Q P T L
  R L I P H C T M A C G H D R H G
  G O T H E S H O U L D R L O L I
  S E F R M D O P L D P V Y A M V
  T Q N N L R U Q T I R E C B R E
  O J L E W H T O A L L U T Y P N
  F D E L R D L U R C A Y M L S V
  Y R F D S O P T W I L L B E C J
  O E I R T L U R V F J D A K W Y
  U M N S L H X S G A R E W C R L
  L T D J N A L D L N C Y R V K O
  N G I V E S Y M E Y P W D A T S
        N C R K C L R U Q H K C
        G R I L R T W C G O D L
```

IF ANY	GOD	FINDING
OF YOU	WHO	FAULT
LACKS	GIVES	AND IT
WISDOM	GENEROUSLY	WILL BE
HE SHOULD	TO ALL	GIVEN
ASK	WITHOUT	TO HIM

James 1:5_____

_____

A Faithful Father

James 4:8

To put the following words in the right order, start at the beginning of each rope and follow it to the correct blank line.

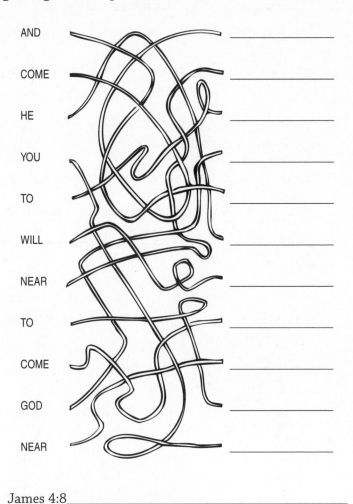

AND   _____

COME   _____

HE   _____

YOU   _____

TO   _____

WILL   _____

NEAR   _____

TO   _____

COME   _____

GOD   _____

NEAR   _____

James 4:8_____

_____

_____

Great Bible Jokes and Riddles #4

1. What kind of soap does God use to keep the oceans clean?

2. What kind of lights did Noah have on the ark?

3. Why did the giant fish finally let Jonah go?

4. Which animals on Noah's ark had the highest level of intelligence?

5. How many books in the Old Testament were named after Ruth?

6. How do you know buses were used in Bible times?

7. Which of the Old Testament prophets were blind?

8. What two things could the apostle Paul never eat for breakfast?

9. Samson was the strongest man who ever lived, but there was one very light thing he could never hold for very long. What was it?

10. If Moses would have dropped his rod in the Red Sea, what would it have become?

Always Ready to Forgive
1 John 1:9

If we tell God we are sorry for our sins, He will forgive us. He will never change His mind, and He will never remind us of our past sins. God's forgiveness is forever!

The verse below is written in secret code. Use the code key to figure out which letters to write above the numbers. For example, number 25 is the letter "A."

```
 7  4      21  3       1 13 12  4  3 17 17

13 19 16      17  7 12 17      6  3       7 17

 4 25  7 18  6  4 19 10      25 12  2       8 19 17 18

25 12  2      21  7 10 10       4 13 16  5  7 20  3

19 17      13 19 16      17  7 12 17

25 12  2      14 19 16  7  4 23

19 17       4 16 13 11      25 10 10

19 12 16  7  5  6 18  3 13 17 12  3 17 17
```

Code key:

A	B	C	D	E	F	G	H	I	J	K
25	26	1	2	3	4	5	6	7	8	9

L	M	N	O	P	Q	R	S	T	U	V
10	11	12	13	14	15	16	17	18	19	20

W	X	Y	Z
21	22	23	24

1 John 1:9 _____

_____

A New Heaven and New Earth

Revelation 21:1–22:6

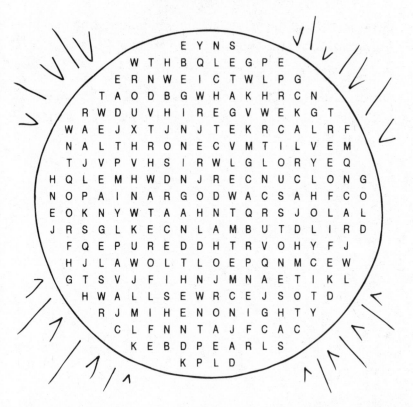

ALPHA AND OMEGA
BEGINNING AND THE END
GLORY
GOD
GOLD
HOLY CITY
LAMB
LIGHT

NEW EARTH
NEW HEAVEN
NEW JERUSALEM
NO DEATH
NO NIGHT
NO PAIN
NO SEA
PEARLS

PRECIOUS STONES
PURE
THRONE
TREE OF LIFE
TWELVE ANGELS
TWELVE GATES
WALLS
WATER OF LIFE

Jesus, Our King Forever

Revelation 22:13

Jesus has always been and always will be the King of our universe. We are the children of the greatest King of all!

Can you break the secret code and find out what Revelation 22:13 says? Use the code key to figure out which letters should go on the blank lines below. For example, number 20 is the letter "A."

```
 __        __  __       __  __  __       __  __  __  __  __
  2        20   6       13   1  24       20   5   9   1  20

 __  __  __       __  __  __       __  __  __  __  __
 20   7  23       13   1  24        8   6  24  25  20

 __  __  __       __  __  __  __  __       __  __  __
 12   1  24       25   2  11  12  13       20   7  23

   __  __  __       __  __  __  __       __  __  __
   13   1  24        5  20  12  13       13   1  24

 __  __  __  __  __  __  __  __  __       __  __  __
 21  24  26   2   7   7   2   7  26       20   7  23

          __  __  __       __  __  __
          13   1  24       24   7  23
```

Code key:

A	B	C	D	E	F	G	H	I	J	K
20	21	22	23	24	25	26	1	2	3	4

L	M	N	O	P	Q	R	S	T	U	V
5	6	7	8	9	10	11	12	13	14	15

W	X	Y	Z
16	17	18	19

Revelation 22:13 _____

_____

_____

Whodunit?

1. Who wrote in the sand with His finger?

2. Who was the wisest man on earth?

3. Who was the strongest man ever?

4. Which two men in the Bible never died?

5. Who told an Egyptian king to "let my people go"?

6. Who was the queen that saved all the Jews of Israel?

7. Who baptized Jesus?

8. Who preached the Sermon on the Mount?

9. What king of Israel played the harp?

10. Who helped the man who had been robbed, beaten, and left for dead along a road?

Jesus Is Coming Again!
Revelation 22:12

Right now Jesus lives in heaven. But there is coming a day when He will return to earth to set up a beautiful and perfect kingdom for us to live in. What a wonderful day that will be, for from that time onward, we will live with Him forever!

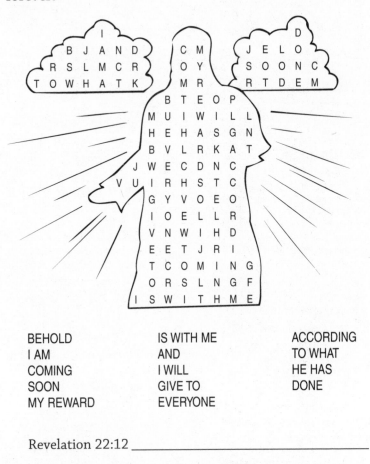

BEHOLD
I AM
COMING
SOON
MY REWARD

IS WITH ME
AND
I WILL
GIVE TO
EVERYONE

ACCORDING
TO WHAT
HE HAS
DONE

Revelation 22:12 _____

_____

_____

Page 9
God's Promise to Abraham

Genesis 12:2—I will make you into a great nation and I will bless you; I will make your name great.

Page 12
Great Bible Jokes and Riddles #1

1. Adam—he was the first in the human race
2. Because David rocked Goliath to sleep!
3. Joseph—because Pharaoh made a ruler out of him
4. Joshua the son of Nun
5. He broke the Ten Commandments all at once
6. Where the Lord gave Moses two tablets
7. On the head
8. "Go easy on the bait, boys. I have only two worms."
9. Samson—he brought the house down
10. Saturday and Sunday—the rest are all week (weak) days

Page 21
Fun with Numbers #1

1. Six: He rested on the seventh day (Genesis 2:2)
2. Forty (Genesis 7:12)
3. Twelve (Genesis 49:28)
4. Forty days (Matthew 4:1-2)
5. Two (Luke 21:2)
6. Twelve (Deuteronomy 1:22-23)
7. Forty (Numbers 14:34)
8. Seven (Joshua 6:15)
9. Twelve (Matthew 10:1)
10. One hundred and twenty years (Genesis 6:3)

Page 22
The Twelve Tribes of Israel

1. Asher
2. Dan
3. Issachar
4. Joseph
5. Napthali
6. Simeon
7. Benjamin
8. Gad
9. Judah
10. Levi
11. Reuben
12. Zebulun

Page 23
The Key to True Success

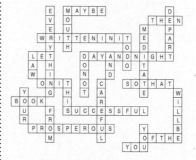

Joshua 1:8—Do not let this Book of the Law depart from your mouth: meditate on it day and night, so that you may be careful to do everything written in it. Then you will be prosperous and successful.

Page 29
God Is Worthy of Our Worship

1 Chronicles 16:25—Great is the LORD and most worthy of praise; he is to be feared above all gods.

Page 30

Which Came First? #1

1. Job
2. Vashti (Esther 1:19; 2:17)
3. Jesus turning water into wine (John 2:1-11; 6:1-14)
4. King Saul (1 Samuel 10:24; 1 Kings 1:39)
5. Esau (Genesis 25:25-26)
6. Jesus' arrest (John 18:12; 18:15-27)
7. The shepherds (Luke 2:8-12; Matthew 2:10-11)
8. Cain (Genesis 4:1-2)
9. The Philistines (Joshua 13:3; Matthew 23)
10. Noah (Genesis 6; Exodus 2)

Page 33

He Protects You

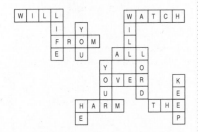

Psalm 121:7—The LORD will keep you from all harm—he will watch over your life.

Page 39

Great Bible Jokes and Riddles #2

1. When Joseph served in Pharaoh's court
2. The elephant. He took his trunk while the fox and the rooster took only a brush and comb
3. When Rebekah walked to the well with a pitcher, and when the prodigal son made a home run

4. Because Noah sat on the deck
5. The widow's "mites" and the "wicked flee" (Mark 12:42; Proverbs 28:1)
6. When God divided the light from the darkness (Genesis 1:4)
7. In Acts 1:14—"These all continued with one accord" (NKJV)
8. His father was Enoch, who didn't die because he was taken directly to heaven (Genesis 5:24)
9. Yes. The duck took a bill, the frog took a greenback, and the skunk took a scent
10. Tyre (tire)

Page 41

God's Great Care for You

Nahum 1:7—The LORD is good, a refuge in times of trouble. He cares for those who trust in him.

Page 48

The Amazing Life of Jesus

1. John the Baptist (Matthew 3:13-15)
2. Forty days (Mark 1:13)
3. Twelve (Luke 6:13)
4. The narrow gate (Matthew 7:13-14)
5. Ninty-nine (Luke 15:3-7)
6. Love them (Matthew 5:44)
7. Two fish and five loaves of bread (Matthew 14:19)
8. The Sea of Galilee (John 6:1, 16-19)
9. Zacchaeus (Luke 19:2-4)
10. A donkey's colt (Mark 11:1-11)

Page 49

The Lamb of God

John 1:29—John saw Jesus coming toward him and said, "Look, the Lamb of God, who takes away the sin of the world!"

Page 52
Jesus' Miracles

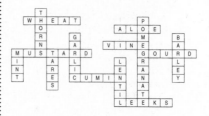

Page 54
The Great Shepherd

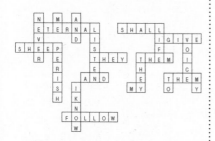

John 10:27-28—My sheep listen to my voice; I know them, and they follow me. I give them eternal life, and they shall never perish.

Page 56
Jesus Is the Only Way

John 14:6—I am the way and the truth and the life. No one comes to the Father except through me.

Page 63
Plants of the Bible

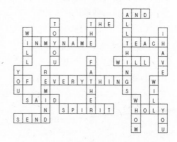

Page 65
Which Came First? #2

1. John the Baptist (Luke 1:35-36)
2. Rebekah (Genesis 24; 29)
3. Ruth (Ruth; Esther)
4. Joseph (Genesis 37-50; Joshua)
5. The flood (Genesis 6-8; 11:1-9)
6. King David (1 Samuel 16:11-13; Jeremiah)
7. Moses at the burning bush (Exodus 3:1-6; Exodus 20:1-17)
8. Jesus being baptized (Matthew 3:13-15; 14:25)
9. Adam (Genesis 2; Genesis 12)
10. Jesus' baptism (Matthew 3:13-16)

Page 66
The Holy Spirit Is Your Teacher

John 14:26—The Holy Spirit, whom the Father will send in my name, will teach you all things and will remind you of everything I have said to you.

Page 71
First and Last

1. Cain (Genesis 4:1)
2. Adam (Genesis 2:20)
3. Saul (1 Samuel 10:21-25)
4. Eve (Genesis 4:1-2)
5. "It is finished" (John 19:30)
6. Genesis
7. Matthew
8. Revelation
9. The water turned to blood (Exodus 7:19-20)
10. Turning water into wine (John 2:1-11)

Page 74
What's the Missing Word? #1

1. always (Philippians 4:4)
2. strength (Philippians 4:13)
3. heart (Psalm 139:23)
4. Word (John 1:1)
5. world (Mark 16:15)
6. yesterday (Hebrews 13:8)
7. obey (Colossians 3:20)
8. again (John 3:7)
9. neighbor (Galatians 5:14)
10. heart (Matthew 22:37)

Page 75
A Free Gift

Romans 6:23—The wages of sin is death, but the gift of God is eternal life in Christ Jeus our Lord.

Page 77
Your Heart, the Spirit's Home

1 Corinthians 6:19—Your body is a temple of the Holy Spirit, who is in you.

Page 78
A Way Out of Temptation

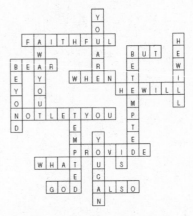

1 Corinthians 10:13—God is faithful; he will not let you be tempted beyond what you can bear. But when you are tempted, he will also provide a way out.

Page 80
Doing All to God's Glory

1 Corinthians 10:31—Whether you eat or drink or whatever you do, do it all for the glory of God.

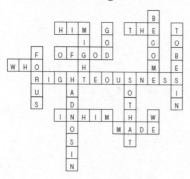

Page 82
From Sin to Righteousness

2 Corinthians 5:21—God made him who had no sin to be sin for us, so that in him we might become the righteousness of God.

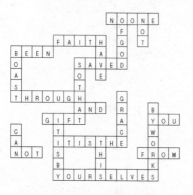

Page 84
Saved by Grace Alone

Ephesians 2:8-9—It is by grace you have been saved, through faith—and this not from yourselves, it is the gift of God—not by works, so that no one can boast.

Page 85
Great Bible Jokes and Riddles #3

1. No, he came forth (fourth) out of the ark
2. The letters *m* and *a*
3. At the banks of the Jordan
4. Eve, when she gave Adam a little Cain
5. Grandparents
6. A little before Eve
7. The story about the fellow who loafs and fishes
8. None; Moses didn't take the animals on the ark—Noah did
9. Because it had no Eve
10. His promises

Page 86
Loving Your Parents

Ephesians 6:1—Children, obey your parents in the Lord, for this is right.

Page 87
Serving Other People

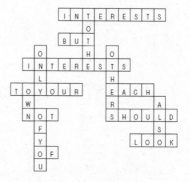

Philippians 2:4—Each of you should look not only to your own interests, but also to the interests of others.

Page 89
The Right Kinds of Thoughts

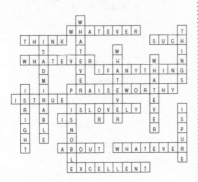

Philippians 4:8—Whatever is true, whatever is noble, whatever is right, whatever is pure, whatever is lovely, whatever is admirable—if anything is excellent or praiseworthy—think about such things.

Page 90
What's the Missing Word? #2

1. first (Matthew 6:33)
2. Shepherd (Psalm 23:1)
3. way (John 14:6)
4. life (John 11:25)
5. faith (Ephesians 2:8)
6. heart (Psalm 119:11)
7. lamp (Psalm 119:105)
8. light (Matthew 5:14)
9. world (John 3:16)
10. eternal (John 3:15)

Page 93
Our Guide to the Christian Life

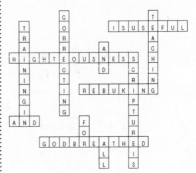

2 Timothy 3:16—All Scripture is God-breathed and is useful for teaching, rebuking, correcting and training in righteousness.

Page 95
Fun with Numbers #2

1. Two (Genesis 2:15,22)
2. Seventy (Jeremiah 25:11)
3. Sixty-six books
4. Twelve (Genesis 49:1,28)
5. Three (Jonah 1:17)
6. Ten (Exodus 7–12)
7. Two (Matthew 27:38)
8. Three (Daniel 6:10)
9. About 5,000 people (Matthew 14:21)
10. Thirty (Matthew 26:14-15)

Page 96
Jesus Never Changes

Hebrews 13:8—Jesus Christ is the same yesterday and today and forever.

Page 98

A Faithful Father

James 4:8—Come near to God and he will come near to you.

Page 99

Great Bible Jokes and Riddles #4

1. Tide
2. Floodlights
3. Because he couldn't stomach him
4. The giraffes, they were the tallest
5. Thirty-one—the rest were named before Ruth
6. Because Proverbs 30:31 mentions greyhound
7. Ezra, Hosea, Joel, Amos, Jonah, Nahum, and Habakkuk—none of them had i's
8. Lunch and supper
9. His breath
10. Wet

Page 100

Always Ready to Forgive

1 John 1:9—If we confess our sins, he is faithful and just and will forgive us our sins and purify us from all unrighteousness.

Page 102

Jesus, Our King Forever

Revelation 22:13—I am the Alpha and the Omega, the First and the Last, the Beginning and the End.

Page 103

Whodunit?

1. Jesus (John 8:6-8)
2. Solomon (1 Kings 3:12)
3. Samson (Judges 15:14; 16:5)
4. Enoch and Elijah (Genesis 5:24; 2 Kings 2:11-12)
5. Moses and Aaron (Exodus 5:1)
6. Esther (Esther 7:3)
7. John the Baptist (Matthew 3:13-15)
8. Jesus (Matthew 5–7)
9. David (1 Samuel 16:18-19)
10. A Samaritan (Luke 10:33-35)

If you would like to contact Steve and Becky Miller
with inquiries about the puzzles in this book,
you can do so at
srmbooks@comcast.net